Let's Talk About

BEING FAIR

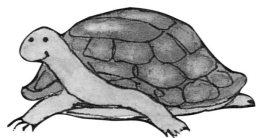

AN EARLY SOCIAL SKILLS BOOK

Written by Joy Berry   **Illustrated by Roey**

GOLD STAR PUBLISHING ™

Hello, my name is George.
I'd like to tell you a story
about my friend, Sam.

This is Sam.
Sometimes Sam wants something
that is unfair for him to have.

3

Like Sam, sometimes you might want something that is unfair for you to have.

5

Sometimes you might unfairly want to do something or to go somewhere.

7

Sometimes you might unfairly want another person to do something for you.

8

9

It is fair for you to get some of the things that you want. However, it is not fair for you to get what you want if it will harm you.

10

It is not fair for you to get what you want if it will harm another person.

13

It is not fair for you to get what you want if it means that something will be damaged or destroyed.

15

It is not OK to get what you want if it is not fair for you to get it.
- You should not take something that belongs to someone else.
- You should not take more than your fair share of something.
- You should not take something if it is not your turn to take it.

There are things that you can do to make sure that you get whatever is fair for you to have.
Don't expect to get something for nothing. Find out what you need to do to get what you want. Then do those things.

19

Be clear when you ask for something.
Say exactly
• what you want,
• why you want it, and
• when and where you want it.

21

Be polite when you ask for something.
Use a calm, polite tone of voice when
you speak.
Begin every request with words such as:
• "May I please…?" or
• "Will you please…?"

23

Be gracious when a person agrees
to give you what you want.
Tell the person, "Thank you."
Then do whatever you have
agreed to do in exchange for
what you want.

Thank you for taking
me to get my kite and
for paying for half.
I'll get my half of the
money out of my
piggy bank.

Try not to ask for something more than two times. You make your request known when you ask for something the first time.
Ask for something a second time only if the other person did not hear you or understand your request.

27

You are annoying people when you ask for something three or more times.
When you annoy people, they often get angry at you.
When people get angry at you, it is almost certain that they will not give you what you want.

29

Try to accept it when a person says, "No."

The nicer you are to a person who has told you, "No," the more likely it is that the person will say, "Yes" the next time you make a request.

31

Remember this:
Being fair is the best way to get
the things that you want or need.